You Remind Me of
Marilyn Monroe

Also by Steven Berkoff

Short Story Collections
Gross Intrusion
Graft: Tales of an Actor

Dramatic Works
Plays 1: West, East, Greek, Sink the Belgrano, Massage,
Lunch, Bow of Ulysses, Sturm und Drang
Plays 2: Decadence, Kvetch Acapulco, Harry's
Christmas, Brighton Beach Scumbags, Darling You
Were Marvellous, Dog, Actor
Plays 3: Ritual in Blood, Messiah, Oedipus – The Secret
Love-Life of Ophelia,
Requiem For Ground Zero

Adaptations
Aeschylus, Poe and Kafka,
Agamemnon, The Fall of the House of Usher,
The Trial, Metamorphosis, In the Penal Colony

Production Journals
A Prisoner in Rio
I Am Hamlet
Meditations on Metamorphosis
Coriolanus in Deutschland

Autobiography
Free Association

Photographic History
The Theatre of Steven Berkoff

Travel Writings, Essays and Poetry Collections
Shopping in the Santa Monica Mall
America
Overview
My Life in Food

You Remind Me of Marilyn Monroe

Love
Journeys
Loneliness

◕

STEVEN BERKOFF

HERLA

Published by
HERLA PUBLISHING, an imprint of

ALMA BOOKS LTD
London House
243–253 Lower Mortlake Road
Richmond
Surrey TW9 2LL
United Kingdom
www.almabooks.com

You Remind Me of Marilyn Monroe first published by Herla in 2009
Copyright © Steven Berkoff, 2009

Steven Berkoff asserts his moral right to be identified as the author of
this work in accordance with the Copyright, Designs and Patents Act
1988

Printed in UK by CPI Antony Rowe

ISBN: 978-1-84688-079-7

Contents

No One   3

She   7

What a Waste   9

Nothing Can Take That Away   11

The Kiss   13

Scroll of Agony   16

You Remind Me of Marilyn Monroe   19

Compromise   21

Get out   23

Pain   26

Finish, No Hate   28

Hate   30

Hell in L.A. February 1981   31

Hell (in London)   32

For Men   37

Jocasta's Loss   39

The Tree   43

Actor   45

Black Skater   55

Action   57

Californian Morn   58

Baby Talk   61

You Remind Me of
Marilyn Monroe

No One

No one in the world feels like you
No one in the world is like you
No one in the world holds you as I do
No one in the world is as tasty as you
No one in the world holds me as you do
No one in the world feels just right like you
No one's arse feels just right like yours
When I hug it from behind that special
Soft feel through my thighs and groin
Standing at the sink I put my arm around
Your waist and nuzzle in your ear and press
Myself against the soft part of my dear
My golden child, my brat and woman wild
No one in the world talks like you
No one has that soothing silky brew
That sound of satin ticking round
My ears love hungry for only your words
Cause no one in the world tastes so sweet
Like you, no one has that gift for words
Each dipped in honey before you drop them
In my ears and slither deep inside my mind
Where no one in the world looks like you
Child woman, nymph, adult, baby bear. Whatever
You want to be I will be there. Be a brat
A beast, a wanton slut, be a nun, priestess
Or fat pup, be a saint, a whore, a sick old
Thing, just be mine. You be anything
Cause no one in the world holds me like you
Do. No one since the end of time since I
Came screaming in into this world of mine. No
One held me like I was precious velvet
No one has held me like I was a peach to eat
No one held me like a manly treat
No one in the world, in the whole vast aching

Seething, heaving, thumping humping world
Has squeezed and touched my manhood just like
You, like you loved that part of me… no one
Made me feel female and surrender like that.
No one has felt as sweet as you, no one fits
Me as you do… no one seems as a garden, so
Clean and pure, so full of sheen, so sweet and
Wholesome, I dive into a sea of flesh and warm
And hold you tight hold your head in the night,
Hold on to you and press my force into your
Groin, like it was, as if to join us for eternity…
Not just for now. I want to leave my seed in
You to grow. I want to see the fruits of our
Strong love a baby you or a baby me or just
A baby we. So that in loving me I leave
My love in you cause no one in the world touched
Me like you do when in the car your arm decides
To test your wanton man and knowing that no one
In the world feels like me my blood flows free
Responding to your touch cause no one in the world
Claims me that much. Just no one, no one in the
World has eyes like yours, no one in the world
Has drunk them up as I do and loved you in the
Night and in the morn, I love you on waking and
You wake so sweet to say your honeypot needs
Its treat. Wakes me to say darling hold me tight
Wakes me to say I love you, in the night. Wakes
Me to say kiss kiss bright man, a body sculptured
To fit yours just right. Wakes me to say this love is
Ours… wakes me… wakes me to unmake me.
I roll over and open my thighs… spread my right
Leg over yours feel my knees digging the
Bed… my joints and spine curves my arse in the
Air. I rise and fall like a wave, like the crash
As the wave rises up and lets itself collapse…
Cause no one feels quite like you… no one cause

4

Love penetrates through and eats into the heart
Feels comfortable and will not part from that
Place... so I rise and fall like a wave like the
Wind through the grass sending its ripple through
Cause no one in the world has ever felt like you...
No one in the world smiles as you do... your smile
Eats right inside my heart, your kiss is the
Membrane of it... your soft "five-second slow one"
And you suck it out my breath for every kiss
You take I make another ten. Cause no one in
The world has your soft lips... no one... is it
Possible to be so soft... is it true... is it real.
Are your knees the schoolgirl I try to please...
My embryo of childhood... soft fissure in your
Groin, the lake of womanhood I want to join.
No one in the world stands like you when you
One hand on your hip, one foot on its ball and
One on its heel. Who watches you so much and
Wants to feel every move that you make.
I take my mental pictures every day.
Racing womanhood before the ocean on your skates...
Little mercury, fluting Peter Pan whizzing through
Space... followed by your wobbly man. So don't,
Because no one in the world, so don't, because no one
In the world loves like you. Hold on to me and I'll hold on
To you. I'll question the sands. I'll look into time...
I'll understand your needs and worldly drive.
I'll understand it all now from whence it sprung,
Understand the aching need just to belong. But no one in
The world has made me feel like you... no one in the world
Has made a kiss feel like a little trace of heaven... a little
Bliss. No one grips my hand like you when at that
Moment when the world stands still and I deliver my
Seed to you to sweeten and soften your needing womb
Cause no one, but no one makes me feel so proud. No
One but no one, I'll hurl your name at the clouds... no one

In the world… no one in the bright, big majestic,
Pounding, arse-licking, preposterous, amazing
World has made me feel like you do. Alive! Alive! A giant
Walks, my heart expands. I am happy to be a man, cause
No one, just absolutely not one singly itsy-bitsy human
Soul has me feel this way cause no one in the world is
Like you.

She

Take me home oh God take me home oh God where
amidst the dandelions, the ochre pots where avocado
pips rest in the nascent stage a little water
just a drop to rest their bums in, their flesh the last
night's salad in the cool of evening's love, where she...
oh Christ have mercy on those that need
where she, did you once see a face coming to you
from outer space where she, Jesus, with hands
outstretched she would greet thee after work.
You're coming down the street. She at the door
She turns and hands and arms outstretched she
Welcomes you, where you and she, don't think about it
He the hard, the separated yolk the parted shattered
egg of love that lies never to be remade,
He the ache of the hard "H" that needs the
"SH" of she to make the softer part of the human face.
He, hard, bone, alone, cold as a silent telephone,
Needing the softness of the "SH" of she where once in
the cool of evening's love you'd eat the fruits of earth
together in the soft and fragrant night her soft she in the
room carving out S's and warm round curves as she
would make the salad and in the cool round soft curved
evening air that she shaped out with her moving curves,
the cat would purr and together we were a pair
together, we just were, don't think about it
Take me home, oh God where amidst the smell of hair
and special ointments women need somehow to clean
the torrid city air their frail and tinsel rags that seem as
thin as moth-soft wings hang in the wardrobe with her
blood's air and warmth of woman smell.
That special odour like the earth or bread or
greengages or seashells. Or just the smell of her, the she,
odour of birth and aching she, odour unlike the male
hard ache that's more a pain when separate from the
soothing balm that changes pain to ecstasy and curving
bodies in the lair where lion and lioness mate, pair of

7

sleeping bodies he a chair an "s" for her to nestle in
He, a crest or crooked mass of flesh that she pours
All her flesh around and moulds her parts in his.
Her bum all soft and round in groin.
Her arm round shoulders in the nest of his bony
hairy chest her hair tickling his nose like cobwebs in
the air her thighs soften his marble knees.
Two in one he gives his he to she and she to he
The hard to soft the pain to ecstasy.
Don't think about it now oh God
Days squandered in the doubts and fears to enter
perfumed gardens, exchange the empty hard-lined
walls, dead room with TV deadly cathode rays
exchange for she-filled days
Don't think of how it was don't carry her smile a mile
high in the centre of your eye her teeth and lips lit up
The sky, don't think about it grab a cigarette
don't listen for her laugh in the bitterness of empty
nights, a musical cadenza that smote the silence,
flute of life-joy in the female throat
the female sound the high and rising stark animal joy.
Don't think about her touch no, not that not so much
that's the worst thing grab a cigarette and numb that
sting, her fingers around yours, her fleshy rings
her small soft hands, don't think about that don't,
holding yours as you, walking together don't, please
don't think, and resting in the lazy grass her head on
your lap no God, no don't, the way a woman rests her
head so trustingly in her man's groin don't think about it
now! And making plans you never made as she chews
upon a blade, you, sheltering your eyes from the sun's
hard blaze. Are you crazy, don't think, don't kid yourself
with thoughts that stink, her crimpled cotton dress alive
with printed flowers. Don't kill yourself with thoughts that
kill and you had the moment, had the world, had her.
Time stopped still and waited... but then you... what did
you do? No, no, no don't, you hesitated.

What a Waste

So I pace around put on the tea, smoke a fag, have a
pee, go to the café eat my toast, pay the bill and face the
most horrible grey and turgid sky. It pains to look it in
the eye so keep my downtrod face away from horror
shows that pass all day for life in this town's damp decay.
Winter eats my heart away, hours are rats of empty days.
They chew the lonely minutes away, each hour that is not
filled with joy or love is spilled upon the floor of pain,
The rug grows thicker every day, each day that is not
filled with love becomes a rat feeding on the dung that
one useless unfilled day becomes, the dreams come
then to haunt the nights, the days lay broken dead unripe.
Beside the bed which used to be a ship we two
would sail into the dark streams of our fantasy
And play and so, what is it now? An unmarked grave I
climb all stinking into my pit my unmade coffin smelling
foul of fags. Unexercised no fresh mouth needed for no
mate to kiss and maybe copulate or just caress.
What for, why live an old decaying bore?
Who sleeps alone behind a door, the night then takes
its toll like box and cox, the night shift working now
and hurls more rocks into my brain? And forehead
sweats, it's her again, a rerun of the dreams that give
me such awful shitty pain. The night recedes just as the
day fades in and light brings on another pain another
day oh God another day of shit tormented emptiness,
Another phrase in the long sentence for some
crime, what did I do God be my judge? What did I do
this time? Don't let the day come yet.
Don't let the aching light show age and wrinkles in
my bed. Don't let the light show some lonely piece
of man in bed. Don't waste your light on this foul lump
of flesh. Don't expose to Heaven's eye a single lonely
man who cried. What did I do oh God?

9

What did I do? Like small bent hairpin alone in
sorrowed bed. But yet it comes, the dawn it groans to
see what living torment there is in bone and flesh, in
every room another hairpin starts to move its weight
of agony from room to room. Kettles move as if by
habit's need, don't want to but do something just to
breathe, make your small single cup of tea. Once,
some time ago he made two cups. Had a reason to get
up and go. Had a cause when light filtered through the
shuttered claws of wooden slats.
And see his mate sleeping like a cat all soft and warm
like buttered toast and marmalade.
Had reason to get up and make the most from each
minute of their brief lives.
To tiptoe in the kitchen make the brew of red-bush she
was used to, bring it in all steaming in two cups.
Had reason then to get up and rouse the sleeping
beauty with the taste of man, husband and lover.
Brief span. What a waste
When I see the heap of loveless world in a haste
dragging their heavy unloved souls around the streets.
What a waste when our hearts to our love did leap.
What a waste. I see dead souls in the trains and buses
in cafés all loveless looking grey
The shade of unloved flesh that lonely stain
What a waste.

Nothing Can Take That Away

Nothing can take away
You sitting on my lap
Like some big grown-up
Schoolgirl, sweet as honey
Thrusting your cunt at me
You randy monkey pulling
Your knickers to one side
And sweetly letting your
Bum and hips slide down
Over your guy

Nothing can take that
Away from me, my sweet
Angel sitting across my
Knee and safe and strong
In my caress, your skirt
Pulled up, your woman's tenderness
Your love for me without duress
Given open, legs apart and
Heaving your whole being
Onto my part

The part that always was alive
To you, the part that showed
My love for you was true
That stood up to attention
When his queen bestowed a
Soft touch on her king
Or even some sweet word was
Fuel enough to make it hard
Just your sweet mouth and
Soft and tender sounds
Nothing can take that away

Would light me up and make
It stand up proud
Nothing can take away
From me your crying eyes
And pour your cum in me
You'd cry that day when
Melting you would need
Your man inside who made
You bleed. Nothing in the world

Not all the words you make
To build a prison round
Your mate, can make me
Doubt the love, the sweetheart
Felt caress the lion feels
For lioness, nothing can take
Away the hold, the touch, the
Feel, the squeeze and soft embrace
The wake-up in the night
When rising from your sleep
And

Hold me – hold me tight: see how it feels
Feel how hot it burns, my honeypot, not lustful
but in love
For one who sleeping by
Your side would wake and
Like a mate relieve his
honeyed bride. Nothing
Just nothing will take that away

The Kiss

Most of all in the night, suddenly feeling
desperately alone I awoke, forgetting for the
moment as I surface through the clouds of a
dream. Forgetting that my mate lay next to me,
my mate sleeping beside me... I turned to face
her suddenly, and in that one desperate second of
loneliness I turn to hold her fast but firm in my arms
and kiss her, I had in my dream been away as if a
thousand years away and in that one desperate
second I rushed to seize her as if I had returned
home from a desperate voyage.

She wakes in the still lake of her sleep that had so
abruptly shattered. I plunged into these calm waters
of her sleep and sent waves billowing across the
stillness and she is rocked by waves into wakefulness.

I kissed her astounded at my need to find her mouth
which did not disappear like a dream but responded
and was firm and soft and fondant and replied. I
kissed her suddenly and strongly; is this beautiful
woman lying next to you in all her perfumed
loveliness, the perfume of her own body's sweet
musky smells, is she yours... to kiss her in a rush
in the urgency of my loneliness having forgotten in
the blistering awfulness of the dream of my
loneliness, having forgotten in that one awful second
that she was indeed there!

The sudden joy, overwhelming me, that, yes! She is
there and does not vanish into a mist... Oh how the
dream had robbed me of her and left me waking with
still its bitter taste on my lips as dream world overlaps
into real world and for that second of overlap
forgetting, not knowing, it is real.

I kissed her as if after a long absence; saddened by
the dream the kiss becomes sweeter than ever, like
returning to a dear lover, I kiss her as if the life of her
was drawn into me, as if to restore my soul, to fill my
cup the sweet wine of her breath, so I kissed her like
a parched man. Her kisses melted away my
desolation that had been invading me in the dream,
the dream of isolation, the aloneness which is the
absence of her being and her body, that kind of
aloneness. I forgot she was next to me, nothing
existed but the fear and the dream, but as the cloud
lifted I could see her shape and her sleeping face
slowly materialize.

I moved towards her, I turned my body, my mouth
reached up to the spring of her body and I kissed her
and she kissed me as I kissed her in the same force
and gentle pressure and sweet fierceness and awful
longing and I kissed her long and felt her life and her
breath and her blood's warmth and her wetness and
her tenderness and her likewise need in her own
waking before she almost could know in the knowing
sense.

Like her body and her unconscious self almost knew
before the person knew, like she was kissing me
almost before she waked and as she waked found
herself to be kissing me.

It's warm, the clock is ticking, and she is warm next to
you. She lies with shadows and a faint street light
picks up the outer shell of her ear…
Your right hand is around her waist and you draw her
heavenly womanness into you like a magnet, she
comes to you, and she smells sweetly of sleep and
the dormant perfumes of her body begin to rouse ever
so gently as I slightly, oh ever so slightly stirred and
her aromas from the shift of her body softly rise. Her

mouth is upon mine as mine is upon hers and I feel amongst other sensations the inner moist membrane of her lips, there is nothing softer in the world, is there?

Her mouth is sensual, yes but it is saying also, are you here, so happy you are here my love, my dear one, mine, I was lonely for you her mouth seems to say, I was away from you in a mist and I was cold and desolate but now you are here her mouth seems to say and I was back with my mouth as the linguist for my thoughts, I was searching for you and I suck the breath and the life out of you and she clings back to me. Did she sense my call… did it resemble her need.

Did my kiss, so needful, so wanting, so loving for her mouth awake in her a cry of her own, did my cry call out hers from the depth of the lake in which she hung in weightless space. Did my need stir her from the depths to surface quickly, come quickly my love, did she hear the cry from the deep wells of her being.

Like the pang in the heart when you hear an animal in the night that sounds hurt, or a baby in a distant room or the weeping of a woman across the stillness from some bed of misery. Did my cry and need awake in her in all her perfumed sweetness a reciprocal cry… so I kissed her in relief to find that she was after all still there. I held on to her and kissed her hard and fiercely as a man kisses a woman that he not only desires but aches for, and sometimes calls it love when he dares admit it to himself and when he dares admit this thing to be an ache of love then the kisses are never so soft, can anything be so soft as the lips of your mate that you ache for in the middle of the night when awakening from a dream and forgetting in that split moment of time that what you most ache for in the world is right next to you…

Scroll of Agony

I laid my life before you like a scroll of agony, as a
Map of time. It's something that you do as if to say
this land is yours, these are the rivers. Here the shores.
These are the scars from distant wars.
I charted my lines upon my well-worn face and said
This was a smile from my first taste of America in
Hershey's bar days when I was still in knee pants and
my heart was filled with Captain Marvel and Batman
thrills. This was a time when the world was mine
when sorrow and pain was a grown-up game, not
for me. The worrying frown, the bad heartache I
saw that in the window, in my mother's face when
I went to school in New York State.
At the attic window when she waved goodbye
I suddenly felt as if for the first time the slow agony
of a grown-up sigh these are the lakes now full to
overflow the laugh lines take the rivers
The tides they come and go
These are the valleys worn so still and smooth
This was the first and painful love
This was my moment of truth here was first grief
Here the line would start when I lost my first
girlfriend. My twelve-year-old sweetheart. Here's the laughter,
here the lines turn up the first time I laughed up my
guts I giggled and shrieked. I was thirteen years old I
didn't know that we were poor, the streets weren't
paved with gold but full of adventure dark nights and
cold shivering boys in alleyways reluctant to let go of
endless days kissing the girls in grown-up games.
Here's the first traces the first whisper of some care
The lines across the forehead that started somewhere
When I was fifteen wore a blood-red shirt, black tie and
black trousers was a raver and a squirt
who thought he was so clever, boy did I get hurt

There's dad, he stands behind me, my son he'll be OK,
The magistrate. He shakes his head, take three
months he would say three months inside cold walls
when I was still a teen, three months, it turned to four
and I was not sixteen. The frown grew from out that
earth the painful struggle of the grown-up birth the
gnashing teeth of get out to work. The years start rolling
on now with painful new force, the days aren't quite so
long now. I've started on a tour that was to crack the
teenage tender to crack the china cup. My pink and
white scrubbed hero. The little East End tough.
The traces turn to shadows and then to hollow grooves
as pain by pain digs out the flesh, carves out the sorrow
on my teenage head with trowels and shovels until I
bled… inside. The crows feet are the heartbreaks. Each
one left its line. It starts from near my forehead and
works its way right down right down into my cheekbone.
A deadly spread of tracks for everyone I gave my heart
For everyone it cracked, it left its voyage on my teenage
map so here is growth and sorrow.
Here is wisdom and care.
Here worry and sickness
Here frustration fears
Here the hundred jobs so like a ball I'd bounce
And each one dug a deeper pit each took its deadly
ounce. It robbed me of my childhood, it stole my tender
years. It vanquished all my playtime. It made grown-up
salt tears. So here the twenties start now. Now the slow
decade. A wilderness of monkeys leaping in my brain
Where to? How, and what to do where shall I go and
where's the school?
Teach me to be brave. Here the drama starts now.
Starts all fresh again, ten more years will leave their
Scars. And then begin again. Here's my life's ambition
Here's creation's crown to express all your sorrow to set
it all right down in actions, in the heat you burn the

stages with your feats to set alight the town, your blood
you use for ink, your tears you use for words, your
memories will forge them into the piercing swords
That will cut deep and wound them,
That will make them laugh and cry.
You'll hurl your words across the world
They'll leap and dance, they'll shine and twirl
They'll encompass souls as they unfurl,
their scroll of agony
The process was a path into which to shine
a light to truth, the pain into a beam,
to cast a pearl into the stream of all the sorrow
of mankind, here now what is this stain?
What falls from out your eye a drop of human pain?
Is this a liquid sigh? Then use its salt upon your food
and share it with your friends. Its flavour will enhance
your table. The sweets come at the end.

You Remind Me of Marilyn Monroe

You remind me of Marilyn Monroe, a sweet-eyed
Doe... vulnerable and soft. Your shoulder
Crushable white froth that I would gather up
Like milky cotton wool, lips soft, silky sensitive
And cool. Your eyes so blue as fresh-washed
Skies as blue as crystals hung up in the morning
Dew. Your softly hanging tits were fair and
Warm as lullabies and gentle as cows' eyes, I'd
Love to let one pendulous warm breast just flow
Into my mouth like running silk and suck the
Unmilked teat in anticipation of some future
Babies' treat. And then your waist, so slender
And defined, an armful of sweet wine, a space
Of flesh to fill my arms with – nothing less
Would satisfy the emptiness. My left arm
Around you pulling you to me, your bum just
Sweeps away to childhood, pink and scrubbed,
Two babies in a tub they do appear and softly
Crushable, spring-mounted moons, I'd grab
A fistful of the aching flesh and feel its soft
Caress delight my palm. Your arse is just a
Psalm that I would write to Heaven... saying you
Got it right! So strong and yet so female frail...
So powerful and yet so delicate as well, so
Innocent and pink and underneath a sink or
Cornucopia of luscious sins, or raging lusting
Whoring priestess. The lady of lusts nests, yet
So total and open with her man she turns to
Virgin in his eyes or moon's Diana. My leg over
Yours in the night made mesh of hot blood
Limbs entwined like snakes, which coil
Corkscrew round each other as you do me, my
Knees nudging your white hot thighs apart.
Your lovely schoolgirl's knees I'd love to

Squeeze your brilliant cascade of legs, you have
Such sexy sweet delicious pegs, just perfect
And so youthful strong from running in New
Zealand, singing songs in the antipodean
Throng. I loved your feet and calves and toes and
every joint that does compose the whole...
The way you move with me – a sailing boat
Just riding on the sea, your heavy swelling tide
Just under me and flowing into earth and
Stream, I'd love to dig inside your sweaty
Teeming earth your sea-smelt salty spray or
Hay that's stacked in barns or new-mown
Grass after the rain, your velvet pouch of
Scarlet hue open and letting forth its dew so
Sweetly when you feel the man, his silk wand
Pushing open the seam beneath our flowing
Stream of gold. I was a prospector for treasure,
For love's delight, my paradise. So, my sweet-hearted
Doe, my Marilyn Monroe, my schoolboy fantasy, my
Woman's secret treasure trove. I'd fondle every dream
I ever had of strumpet, virgin, schoolgirl grown-up
Amazon. Large, generous, bounteous with lots
To give and more... because you are an endless
Thing. Each season you are a different flavour,
A different hue. Big schoolgirl, pimpled nymph
Pouting and frustrated simpering wimp at
Times. Tears right on the crest of your volcano...
Ready to let drop at every tremor. Your howl
And rain for each and every little pain, so full
You are, so ripe with feeling joy, to squeeze
You, you would burst apart like some over-ripe
Passion fruit or sticky big jam tart, sweet rich
And full to overflow, but that is how I like my
Sweetheart, my sugar sweet Marilyn Monroe.

Compromise

Is this the end oh God? Is this the end?
The doubts and sidelong glances put on smiles
Confessions on the phone to distant friends when
you are out the room. The weary list of what she can
or cannot do. He's around the house I don't feel free
Then endless weighing up the grams of love
against the sand of doubt and each day another
grain is dropped upon the dish. The needle trembles
as it tries to balance but in vain. Another day stretches
out its grey canopy over all the dying, over all the rot that
lay as confused as the day before. Solution there is
none. The wires ripped out, wreckage of the shattered
love lay in bits and pieces on the floor. A murder
undiscovered, the body still upon the carpet.
Murderer in the next room wakes from rack-stretched
night. Wishes it was all a dream, the sun will not purge
nor clean to bone the foul corruption on the floor, clean
out the room get rid of things that lay like stale and
Shattered remnants. Spring-clean your life don't try to
repair old love. A glass once shattered is weaker when
you try to glue its broken fangs together.
Just sweep it up and throw it in the dustbin that's the
place for love, a refuse heap and grow a new plant
From the soil make my body and soul a compost and
watch a new one grow from out the earth enriched with
ancient blood. Too many hurts. Too many knives of
doubt have stabbed the body, cut this way and that
plunged in. Slashed. Accused and every accusation even
small becomes another cut until you're walking
casualties. Afraid to move. Afraid to say. Afraid to reveal
the pictures in our brain. Afraid… to be alone for fear
that this love is the only one, so many wounds draw killer
and his victim close a strange perverted empathy
between opponents, make them lovers in their death tryst,

is this the way an enemy crawled itself into your guts and
grew. You nursed the thing until it revealed itself to you
as cancer. Eating your heart you nursed it, wooed
the monster growth. Pretend it was a flower blossoming
forth.
Afraid to say the word which was the large unspoken C.
Instead you died and kept on dying endlessly
Killing all that's best in you
Killing your life and heart
Killing your soul and spirit
Killing your work and all the things that make you grow
Killing your friends and your ideals
Killing your reason your strength and hope
All dying all around you staring at you with limpid dead
eyes with "why" etched upon their weary sighs and when
all is dead and broke, empty of friends, a tattered empty
bag with that monstrous growth watch how you'll be
chucked into the yard and then be food for worms
and maggots, it's hard yes… penalty for carelessness.

Get out

Get out – get out – it seems a trap then get out go, you
sense the horror, something that stinks, that feeling
unexplained. Steel prison bars seem like a veil from a
distance. A knife just tickling feels like feathers till
It's twisting round your entrails, you feel something. An
atmosphere. An odour of something not quite pure. Then
get out. Even rats sense when the ship's about to even
think of sinking. See the birds flee from a seeming calm
before the crack sends thunderbolts and the bursting rain
shatters the world. Snakes crawl away before the
tremors sensing. Clever they are we shrug and shrug it
off. That sudden shiver when your grave was walked
upon they say. There's something more. Something
not clean, someone who holds or held the symbol of your
heart strings. Held so tight. You feel it when a string
grows loose. You feel it dropped. A puppet not pulled up.
Not functioning so well. The master's mind is somewhere
else. Each one who gives their precious strings is saying
here you drive my heart, here are the reins until we part.
My love trusts you with my most precious part. Until the
end your smile will fuel it. Until the end and your kisses
and embrace will soothe it. Your hands will massage life
into its veins and chambers. So until then here are the
Golden strings. And then you feel each shudder from
above. Each tremor in your partner's soul will tremble
down the precious tiny filaments.
So each who gives his heart in one sense makes the
receiver suddenly a master or a master of the art of
making that part of your wealth, your heart, a happy
place or just a dungeon where a slug lies in the corner.
Neglected and abused, instead could make a haven for
your throbbing red and love-filled cave of pulsing life
force where love flows in rich ruby, hot as coals. Could
make a garden full of well-nursed golden daffodils or

rank vile weeds that thrive in places where neglect
has sewn its barren seeds. So in giving your heart's
garden to your mate, you turn the mate to master or to
monster.
Choose what will it be. Choose carefully. The strings get
caught up in a thick web, not cared for they get tangled,
poor puppet twists and gasps upon the leads. Strangled
throat and arms akimbo. No more dancing free and
trustingly in space, no more dallying on the finger tips of
your love's fancy once so careful and delicate, aware of
such a holy cargo and took care. Now twisted and
throttled. The dance becomes grotesque. The bottled
fury strangled in its throat screams out, so drop the
Strings and let me breathe. Be free. Open your fist which
grips my heart strings, afraid to let go just in case
another puppet will not be so keen to replace this poor
struggling thing. So let me go. Don't dally with my heart
which gasps and pumps in heavy humps of treachery.
A kitten held by some lout by its throat and tearing
at the air with its thin feeble claws, let go. Don't hold it
any more. Give my
strings to a new partner who will carefully manipulate her
touch, make the puppet live and celebrate its act. A
Master of the art of holding hearts by their most precious
parts...

You couldn't drive my heart, you made it sway and lurch
even when you thought it was so good, your art so
Skilled. It seldom did perform its weightless dance
without the sudden pull which snatched its breath away...
That almost killed it every day, but like hope has a prayer
that the next time will be sweet and pure, an effortless
familiar reel and guided by trust, patience and good will.
So you prayed for the day when you could dance your
life away, forget that you had even strings so gentle was
the touch, so easy and familiar was the tug, you hardly

knew that someone else was ruling you or part of your
Empire… your heart. So now get out. Drop me upon the
floor. Dash me upon the ground. I'll bruise and bleed but
at least I will be free. I'll gather up my golden strings, so
worn and grimy, wash them clean and find a good
new mistress for me!

Pain

Pain's the meat that satisfies the empty aching gut,
Don't feed me now, not much not so much that it blunts
the acid slicing through the ventricles where passion lies
and needs the vinegar upon the exposed parts to make
Them quiver as a dart shot in the heart. Makes it bleed
its love wounds into symphonies and bloody words.
Creation lay in conflict and earth's upheaval, witness the
birth in blood rush burst and yell, creations forged from
slashing pain where soul is stretched up to its furthest
rack, determining itself by being filled with soul juice, sad
experience wets the eyes and says the soul's alive.
Its screams of pain are witnesses to say it feels spread-
eagled on the wheel of life so don't try and escape
misfortune's blood knife, it's clean, it cuts. It also cuts
the fat away that grew in self-satisfied contented stew.
The act of compromise and living death, afraid to part,
Afraid to face the fresh air on the wound that cuts right
through air, two quivering halves, two wriggling worms all
Cringing as the light, fresh white sight stings the naked
wounds, the deadly numb used flesh that never wakened
to the acid test of touch had died of dull disuse, afraid to
risk exposure to those rawer parts where truth lay dying.
Afraid to face the night's long vigil. Loneliness. Afraid
lest nothing moves out of the night to claim them
Afraid that silence and the dark enfolds them in a coffin's
trap. Instead cling to each other like limpets on a rock
And mould each other in each other's fear then cancer
seeks avenging rage for live cells caught, trapped in a
cage and not set riot free so don't assuage the pain in
Taking on another to fill in space, afraid of so much
Cosmic emptiness to face. The right one is the one that
Makes you feel alive through pain and groan, moan and
agony, ecstasy is next. If you can make the test, tears and
bitter salt doth stain the face, caustic acid dashes from

the dark holes in your face. The soul's on fire the soul
leaps higher when it has a task to grace its table.
Bitter herbs should be a feast as well as quail's eggs
Those who can stand alone in the vast tomb of empty
Silence will be seen longer than the moth grabbing at the
nearest flame and snuff, it's out.
So pain pierce me. Grip me with your long nails
Release the sweet juice of my flesh so I may taste young,
Live and fresh, so pain, whip me until I shriek, let my voice
rise in pitch until it cracks the sheet of glass. Glass
houses where boredom sleeps, so pain, hurl arrows at
my sombre flesh lest it grow full and fat with soft content
and let my blood be as a river of life to bless another's
strife, so pain, release me from the bonds of safety
more a grave so I may spit the earth out of my mouth
and howl. So pain let me walk hot coals should my feet
grow thick and soft so I might dance not rot in thick
carpets lined with dozy dogs and telly on "Your supper's
ready dear", that's ok too.
That's bliss
But must be earnt when fat of compromise is burnt.

Finish, No Hate

Was it meant to end like this oh God? The bitter tongues
recriminating lash, no walking down the frondy arse
swirled front. Hard words and reruns of old hurts, you did
this to me and you did that and on the petty tit for tat, the
script comes out again, the well-thumbed dog-eared
leaves repeating all the things I didn't and all the crimes I
did if only you'd done this, if only you'd done that, if only I
was made of wire and wax, if only I had a box and not
a heart if only I could take my soul apart, if only all my
love was only yours and not a bit to spare for other's
sores. The love that's snatched from others' plates will
only mortify the one and satiate. The love that's
condemned by another's need with cries of gimme,
gimme all to me, will not be as pure as love that freely gave
contains no rancid drop that might contaminate like some
strange virus till all's rank and foul, a dungheap of
passion and infantile.

So don't accuse now, tongue and finger beating out their
pulse of well-remembered scores and filthy acts as if
some higher court was watching in the wings to pass
their judgement and award you costs, the only judge and
jury is ourselves. The one to pass the judgement, the
other to condemn us to our cells of bitterness and guilt,
jealousy and sloth, hatred to the end, an acid bath to
freshen up our wounds to stop the scab from healing, rip
it off and feel again your torturer's mental tongs so you
might howl out all again the wrongs the world did, self-
pitying songs. Be a good judge at the end and pass no
sentence, say that neither is the guilty one, the judge in
you that can forgive will give you many hours more that
you will live hate-free and light. Forgive each other and
forgive yourselves, forgiveness is divine, hate is for
cellars where rats lurk. Murky tombs covered with

mould not often peered into. It lives with termites in the dark. Hate is the killer in the dark. Hate walks a steady pace to feed on life and pounce to suck your life blood, every ounce. Once in it, it won't so easily slip out. Shut the door before its slimy hand crawls round and turns your mansion into slaughterhouse. So if it is to end, let it end well in blaze of sunset glory after spell of thunder and tempest let there come peace, some calm at last so it will heal all wounds of past. Let it end just as it did begin with love and tenderness and in the rain of tears that will bedew the ground, flowers will surely grow and in each one a memory will glow of golden times, the dark hours will dissolve not being fed instead you'll have a garden... years to come that you will walk through... as friends.

Hate

"Hate… I never knew that word my folks," says Eddie in
Steve Berkoff's *Greek*. But hate that's pure and strong
and rich. Hate that comes from vintage bottles tastes so
clean and white it bites back all the bile. It shreds
through all the fake and artifice like acid eating through
the wedding cake – hate – Oh let me learn to hate for he
who hates knows where the borders are between grovel
and vile, knows when to stop and ask himself, why is my
chin scraping the floor, why does my gut knot in a fist
and try to smile while grimace lurks behind the teeth. So
hate burns all up in a rage – hate that's not afraid to
shout. Not hate hid bursting in cauldrons below souring
and messing up your undertow of nature's wealth… your
spleen and guts and pancreas… your heart and viscera,
most of all your head… but hate that opens up the gates.
Hate that shows itself in passion's pistons working full
blast… hate that coruscates. Yelp, shriek and howl –
hate that bellows – fills your lungs with fire. Hate that
puts the spring back in your spine, bent back so far to
Please – you're staring up your own arsehole. Hate oils
the stiffened whip that was your back… pours adrenaline
Upon those fears that once made you a wreck… a
stormy shroud of fear. So now I learn to hate…
In doing so all the fear and self-loathing escapes and
hate soars out into the air… relieves the trembling shell of
human scum and makes it clean… empty again. Purifies
it, like fire licks clean the bones' corrupted meat, you
start again… your vessel clean and purified… your soul
germ-free and sterilized from the loathsome bacteria of
compromise. Soar again sweet bird… rise aloft and
fly… your hates expelled into the sky where God
snatched up the rotten blast and turned it into golden
dust. Look up and see a meteor streak into the dusk.

Hell in L.A. February 1981

Oh God... oh God... oh God... oh God. Forbid the
streets, forbid the streets forbid the heat the heat the
overwhelming heat the heat. Devouring me,
devouring me, devouring me, devouring me, my
feet, my feet, my aching feet, my aching bruised
and battered feet, the concrete, concrete
smashing flesh and bone and blood, wasting me,
wasting me, eating toes and heels and ankles, calves
and knees, groin, sinews pounding, pounding left and
right, right and left. Walk relentless straightened
murdered streets, the murderers of meat and heart and
lungs. The asphalt blasting mix of heat and street and
siren shriek. Oh God, oh God forbid the monster snakes,
the freeways deathways crushing, twisting me, the roller-
coasters deaths highways. Slabs and slabs of metal
glass and brakes, instructions stab the neon sky, where
to take your piece of suffering ache, which intestine to
suck you down, grind jerk and break. A million, million
faces strange, grip wheels in sweaty hatred haste.
Motherfucker out of my way! The minds' computer etch
their scroll of agony upon the human race. Oh God, oh
God, oh God, oh God, don't walk. Walk. Don't walk.
Walk. Don't walk. Walk. Run. Escape, heartbeats
accelerating ache, pressure cooker, heat and
monster obelisks, temple silos rising greet the smoke-
stained filthy sun that burns the carbon sucked into my
hurting lungs. Run and run the street becomes conveyor
belt that rats run on. Treadmill the more you race it follows
on. The faster, faster it will follow your relentless shadow
killing you... stalking killer sucking you... your blood by
drop by bloody drop. Oh God help me help me oh help.
He can't see me beneath the stinking monoxide pelt. A
dot moving down in hell, a snail leaving its spore among
the city's horrid swell.

Hell (in London)

Sometimes I get so lonely. Like it's a disease you catch.
And then I am alone. One day not having made some
arrangement... Forgetting... Thinking that someone may
call by chance... Leaving it in fate's hand... So to speak... I
find myself alone. It's terrible. It's not being alone. That
can be good... But lonely... Like everything's painful.
Because you can't use your voice or your hands or your
body. You can't use any of yourself and when that
happens you have an ache... In your stomach, and I feel
like a non-being. So since you cant speak. Hold. Make
love. Dance. Play. You die. You drink. You smoke. You
do anything to shut out the pain. I walk around the room.
I turn on the TV... I see a wretched film. Wretched but I'm
frightened to turn it off. And I have to keep smoking.
Keep drinking to fill the hole of emptiness. I read
sometimes but then the words start to dance and I get
sleepy because reading's not what I need. I've read
enough in my life. I want to live. And that is... Hold a
woman and love her. That's the best thing in the world.
That's when I use everything at once. My words and ears
and hands and body. And mind. And then I am
transcended. I arise like the phoenix building society out
of the ashtray of my youth, loneliness is a waste of time.
Loneliness is a solitary profession. You can smell a
lonely person. They stink of something that has an edge
of fear to it. Like a plant not watered curls at the edges. A
bit brown. But the horror of it is feeling like a non-being.
When I'm lonely and sitting in my room I imagine myself
as if from a great height... A tiny figure alone in a tiny
room in a tiny house. Just sitting there. Smoking and
putting the kettle on again or sometimes abusing myself.
That's awful. Where there must be an equally lonely
woman somewhere aching for another lonely man and I
throw my love away. I toss it into the ash bin. I crush my
love in Kleenex. And flush it down the loo... And then I

smoke. And then I turn on the TV. And then I turn it off.
And then I go to bed. And then I smoke in bed. And then
I put it out. And then I look at my watch, Yes it is a
respectable time to be in bed. It's not humiliatingly early.
And then I put out the light. And then I curl up and then I
hold my willy. Not for sex this time. But to cuddle part of me.
Sure I've tried to find someone to share this pool of
loneliness. Sure I have. A hundred times. But they get
out of the pool. Or we both get out. Or. One of us gets
bored. Because loneliness is a disease… You have to
give more to a person, a woman than "take me I'm
lonely". After the sharing and the joy of finding someone
and the knowing, there needs to be something else. I
think so… But each time it ends the loneliness gets
deeper… It's like an acid and each time you go further
into you shell to avoid it. You grow older. Less confident.
You grow anxious. So who likes to meet… Somebody
anxious… So you smooth away the anx… You smile and
suggest a drive down to Brighton. Dinner. Movie… A chat.
An experience of something. But your loneliness has
bitten like acid into your soul. You can hear the acid
sloshing around… A pool of loneliness. Inside. You try to
love or make love. But loves comes from joy. From
excitement. What you give is not love but desperation to
hold on to something warm. And each time its audition
for the role of non-loneliness. So you invariably make a
mess of it. Not just with her. With anyone. It's like a
disease you think there's maybe something wrong with
you. You are prone to these attacks like having migraines
or epilepsy. You wonder when the next attack will come.
But it is more than that. It is a deep-down conviction that
somewhere within you there is something… Inferior…
Unworthy and that exposure will lead to it being
discovered. But it's loneliness that brings it on… This
ugly feeling… And when it's there you're too lonely to do
anything about it… Relieve it. So it's a circle. Vicious. The
weekends and the nights are worse. Sometimes it feels

like alive and death. Since I don't feel alive. Being alive
means living and feeling. Lonely means no one knows
I'm alive except me and the cat… Alone in my room. I
can go out and sit in a café and people will mill around
and that's comforting. For a while. I fill my mouth and fill
my eyes with sights but when hunger is staved off… What
then. I like the mornings cause I wake up and the day
has not yet been etched in loneliness. I start with a fresh
sheet. The same as everyone else. I'm hungry. I have
things to do. Like put the kettle on. Go to work. But if I
have no work then the day hangs over me like a threat
that needs to be filled… Especially on weekends. I look in
my book for someone to ring. But usually it's too late…
They're out or have arranged something. It wasn't
always like this. Oh no. I used to sleep with a woman.
The same one. I had a body to wrap myself around like a
blanket. That's nice. You wake up with another human
being. You walk down the street. You hold hands. You
phone home if you're going to be late. You don't look in
an address book wondering who to phone. You have that
there that is your need and her need. You don't look in
books. I miss holding hands. I miss touching and
kissing. I miss talking to her. Smelling her and making
love. Then she went away. One day I came home and
she had gone. I think she got bored. For me she was
enough but she wanted some social life. I'm not so good
at that. I like to stay in and cook a meal… Listen to music
or watch a movie on TV. Chat a while and go to bed.
That's what I like doing. I find one person quite often
enough… Yes sometimes someone would visit. And then
everyone would talk too loudly about everything that
wasn't important and feel forced to have opinions about
the food in southern Mexico or the state of the nation and
I couldn't get involved. So I'd talk less and less and
eventually I'd shut up. And then they'd ask if I was
alright… Like I was suffering because I couldn't vent
some wisdom on some irrelevant matter and all I wanted

to do was get them out so I could go to bed… And cuddle
my woman. The only good thing about those dinner
parties was that they made the cuddle better by the
sheer relief. I started to read to dread the next one.
When the front doorbell went I'd take a deep breath and
put on a smile and pour out wine and smoke too much.
But I don't do that any more. Cause she isn't here
any more. One day I looked at a card in a window of a
shop. Cards that lonely men look at. So I rang and went
round. She was fat and awful. And the room was filthy. I
went in and the TV was on. It was eleven in the morning.
There were empty bottles and ashtrays everywhere. I
couldn't think of entering her so I asked for a wank. I sat
on the sofa and took out the thing which I had used in
the past for loving my woman. I took it out and she took it
in one hand and jerked away while watching TV. I shut my
eyes and pretended that it was OK. But nothing
happened since it was too awful. I wondered where I was
to have come to this. This was love. This was the fruit of
my past. I've come to collect… This… The sweet deserts
of my life. I paid her and went back to my room. The
phone looked at me like a dead thing and I smoked a
cigarette and sat in my room for a long time. Then I went
downstairs and fed the cat and stroked her a few times. I
then read all the letters I had from my woman during the
times we separated and came together again. And then I
looked at my room and what I was in. A cell. The plates
and cups in the kitchen had piled up in the sink. The
laundry needed taking to the bagwash. There was a fine
from the library for books unreturned and threat of court
action. And a huge tax demand brought about by
neglecting my affairs. I looked through my book for
someone to ring and smoked a cigarette but there was
no one I really wanted to be with except a woman or my
woman. I didn't just want to kill time. I didn't want to read
and I didn't want to watch TV. I didn't want to eat and I
didn't want to sit in the pub and get pissed since all these

were really ways of killing yourself. But over a long period. That's when I thought that this is really honestly worse than death. Much, much worse. This surely is living hell. And I wouldn't expect it to change and someone to phone and rescue me since I knew enough about habits and patterns to see this as a recurring theme. Anyway it was raining and it always seemed to rain. I thought I could jump on a plane and go to Australia, or America but the lonely habit would sooner or later return whether it was sunny, raining, near or far. That's when I took the pills. There was nothing dramatic. I had some valium in the bathroom. About a hundred. I went out and brought a bottle of scotch. I took ten at a time with a swig and felt quite high and then I got violently sick but got over it and felt really good. I took the other fifty with water in case I got sick again. I took several hours to die since my life force must have really been quite strong and put up a hell of a struggle. I was not even discovered for four days since few people ever called round and the odd ring of the phone soon stopped. It was the bailiffs who had come to take my furniture for a debt who discovered me. I don't know how they got in. I watched the mortuary man move my body. They didn't know who to call since I had no living next of kin and didn't leave a note. And so they fumbled through my address book until they found someone who knew I had a brother I hadn't seen for years and didn't particularly like. There were few at the funeral. I felt very tranquil about the whole thing and could watch it all… Like it was a dream. Although I did have a pang about the cat. I hoped the neighbour would look after it. They used to. When my woman and I went to Brighton for the weekend. Do you know I had that cat for fifteen years. Do you think I'll be acceptable here being as it was self-inflicted. You see I'd quite like to meet some people…

For Men

If you cannot hold on to your bird then take a sideways
glance at you. Try to find out some truths about yourself
since birds are desperate looking for a nest, a guy must
be almost a mess before a chick decides to split is best.
She'll put up with almost anything in her desire to gain a
ring, he'll be a pig, inconsiderate, not care a fig, she'll
wash his pants and soothe his brow give her sweet body,
make a secret vow to hold on to the end. So fierce is
nature's call that she will bend her principles, thwart all
her rules, since some deep locked chalice of love, love of
her womb, her life her womanhood makes her have faith
that in the end all will be good. And so she strives,
strives on to keep her love alive, fights for what she
needs, the very seeds of future home must now be
sown, see if the earth she has chosen to plant her shoots
will be barren or rich. She has to test the soil to give it a go,
question the earth, dig and grow some sample vine. See
how the man, the soil of all that she calls "mine" will
harvest this little shoot, this twine. So she imparts her
precious love… she gives it birth, with pain strips herself
naked without strain… says take me I am yours, my soul,
my heart, my family, my frilly drawers, all that too. A
woman's body is not as if for man, a receptacle for
spunk, a spittoon for your lust. For woman. Mostly that is,
there must be trust. She is the frailer thing vulnerable to
unwanted stings of lust or men's careless fling. So when
she says that I am yours here is a gift which any man
could never give, a man who likely most is used to
thanks love and pass the tissues. So here it is, a woman
skinned, wide apart, her legs stretched out. She loves
your cock and now you drink your fill. She trusts your
love and does obey your will. She'll keep you clean and
safe and put good food upon your plate. But in return…
just listen mate to me she says. I must obey the rules of

nature, since eternity the woman is the universal flow,
ruled by the moon, ruled by the undertow of tide. She's
the deep connection to the earth. Her blood-rich monthly
sap reminds of her link with nature, it must obey its ends.
She is the female who creates the tides and flow, creates
the ultimate earth-shattering growth.
This woman must be a wife, a
mother, and energy must be let out. The sea is a great
heaving bitch of goddess nymph, her waves, her breasts
that men with rough and tawny skin will sail upon and
spear and kill the whale and engage in battles nuclear
laced because men have lost their nature's place and
now the ultimate, marooned in space, his toys, his metal-
contained crap. Blast off captain, yes sir up and away,
technology is here to stay. Crashing ideologies will
splatter spray atomic razor blades to have our way and
bury cities in death rays. Because at home and hearth man
lost the deep connection to his earth and roots, severed
the chord that linked his mate to him and made him
contemplate the universe within... her giving birth the
greatest miracle on all the earth, who cares to be a hero,
rule the world, be a king of this and that, little Caesar
doth bestride the narrow seas like a colossal jerk, a prick who
lost his place on earth behind medals, power and dirt. So
do not be a fool, when woman throws her love to you,
embrace it, weave its threads into a tapestry so
intricate, so fine... ne'er to be entwined but blessed,
divine. Not say here's the old pitch, it's done OK before,
don't complain you bitch. But chart some other land,
fertile and new. Dig it all up and water too with love,
devotions, understanding and no strife and then your
flower will plant her seeds, will trust and then... give life!

Jocasta's Loss

I miss him, I miss him madly. I just miss him and all that
is him. All the love that I can summon in the world I want
to give to him. I want to dredge every corner and ounce
of my being and squeeze every drop of love I have and
pour it all over him… how could I love him so much… he is
my man, son, lover, sweetheart, dreaded boy, the ache
in my, and the space unfilled for him, everything that my
hands touch that is not him pains me, everything that I
look at which is not his face and body leaves me barren,
everything I taste which is not his kiss is tasteless,
every event which is the passing of summer or the rites
of spring that is not shared with him becomes a cold
empty thing in my heart, with him it becomes glorious as
the manifestation of God. The sun is a blinding searing
pain and the wind chafes me and the food sickens me
and my sleep becomes an empty journey through a
passage of time that is devoid of him. With him it is a
passing through blissful and soul-feeding hours. With him
it is a journey through a garden of delights and when I
wake up with him I wake up reborn and reformed. I am
changed by being one body with him and as he enters
me he exchanges with me parts of me and I take parts of
him and in the end I don't know where I leave off and he
begins but I know we were part of each other in our love
and I am the garden and he comes to me like a gentle
rain and pours his benediction and I open up. And now
bed is empty… so empty like a tomb and my animal of
love which is like a creature that grew in me and roams
around my body pining like an animal starving for its
love, it haunts and I do hear it screaming in the night.
Those long awful nights that were only made for being at
one with your man as you can never quite be at any time
and not in the same way, as when you are silent and
sunk into the outer world, and so I fell into a fitful sleep

and dreams and the cry of the animal and his howls
haunted my dreams and then I dreamt that he was
kissing me and was warm and next to me as if the
animal had left my body and was warm and breathing
and as I turned he had gone in my dream and I was
afraid and alone. He was dead and gone and never
again would he kiss me and the way that he kissed me
was a special way… he always kissed me like after a long
absence, like lovers kiss when they can't quite believe
that they have found each other again and it is
sweet… like honey, and it is simple. It is the recognition
that I know you and you are mine. You can fuck with a
stranger but there is a special way that lovers kiss
because it's simple, sweet and loving, the way your mouth
goes out to your lover and you purse your lips and isn't it
the softest most delicate part of your whole being and
what is so soft and so delicate as your mouth and you
offer it without restraint and without fear because you
want to pour your breath into him and suck his breath
into yours and what is more gentle and soft than his lips
of your mate and does it matter how he came or from
where… the reality is the now… not the ghosts of the past.

And do the mistakes of our love carry the sin in our
hearts… for ever, no. All there is is this beautiful man
whose eyes I can never tire of and on whose face I can
feast and whose hands I always want and whose voice
caresses me in the still night and the warmth of the blood
surging through his body comforts me and the absence
of that is the absence of the world and the absence of
what is the other half and weren't we reunited in another
time and place over thousands of years, and weren't we
travelling once in tents or were we animals or was he my
lion and I his lioness and didn't we find each other
again after years of searching after years of clawing
other bodies to find that secret key that would unlock the

secret we were meant to find, unlock all those parts of
ourselves that we desperately looked for in the others as
they in us, and didn't we hurl ourselves at the bodies of
the world looking and nearly finding or thinking that we
had. And then one day we did and as we did we found
more and more until we unlocked everything within us,
until we were open as the air with no more secrets, and
within we found a light. And if that had to come from out
of me and then that is how it had to be and our love can
transcend anything in the world, can overcome anything,
even the strong guilt that he tormented himself with,
which made him turn away in shame but our love is like
a pure thing... it is like a light that comes directly to you and
you are bathed in it because it shines on the innermost
secret part of your whole being that he opened, and that
is the holy of the holiest like the great temple. And I want
this light to shine on me or I will shrivel... did the gods
trick us... did the Fates play a game with us to take all that
is most wonderful in the world... it is too wonderful to
last... could it be that the Devil preys on what is most
marvellous since it is so much that it defeats it... could it be
that what is marvellous invokes the envy of the gods
since it becomes godlike and we should be denied it. It is
not for mortal souls as they say lest you become us so it
plays tricks on us and twists our fate and puts stones in
our path that we may trip and lose our way. But we will
pick ourselves up, for our love is not an easy one but we
will not let the Devil defeat us with his tricks and
diversions so jealous is he of our passion. We will not let
him gloat at yet another defeat and victory for him. For
he is the bastard of doubt and wants to be satisfied with
less and aren't all people satisfied with less than they
could have because they have not the courage to
combat the Devil and his evil ways and he played a foul
trick on us and we let him snatch our love from out of our
mouths and gave in like weak and easy captives but now

41

we know his colours and with love and prayer I will
defeat him. We will defeat him. I will not be satisfied with
the trinkets he offers for compensation... I want the light...
I want you in my bed... in my empty tomb I crave you... my
light, my soul, my love, my husband, my son... oh come
back to me... I pray for you in the endless minutes... the
wilderness of minutes and each minute is a tomb for the
time of loving that be crammed into that minute... and
each minute is a grave that takes you further and further
away from me and I fear for the going-out of the light of
all the lights in my life and the dusk is seeping in and my
room becomes grey like a dungeon and cold and I
shrank and became withered being deprived of that
which filled me to overflowing. And I dreamt I became
smaller and smaller and eventually returned to dust
because that is what I was before I was me and the love
of creation breathed life into me and I became woman
and was happy to be a woman for can there be anything
more in the world more marvellous than to be a woman
for if I was not I could never love him and I was created
for him and now I want him back... call him back to me...
call him back to me.

The Tree

Love is a heavy burden to bear alone.
It is a tree in a northern wind outstretched on some black
rock bending its rain-lashed branches against the
freezing shock of winter. A dark silhouette stabs an
angry sky no birds will venture down to shelter or to nest
on this bleak naked thing stretched our like Lear in
wilderness. Its branches, vain pleading arms its fingers
jagged broken claws in constant supplication for the end
of ice-dark dreariness its buds curled tight within as if no
sap will ever rise again. No blood will course through its
long veins to make it flower once again no seed will fall,
reduplicate to give this twisted and gnarled stick a mate
so it bends and breaks, heaves itself against the
heartless cold-blooded sky its blind arms pleading out to
Heaven's eye to bend its sight and warm it with its
golden beams of love make it alive shot through with
burning light, ignite the frozen hard sap and make it melt
course through the hard cold trunk and arms and feed
the tiny buds curled tight like foetuses within their cups.
And when at last the spring comes down one pink
stained dawn to gently rest its soft breath on this tree,
forlorn and heartbroke on its withered blasted heath
It will begin the process and repeat the age-old clock of
time the earth will heave and break as shoots strain up
from deathlike sleep and shake and tremble as juice
begins to take its long journey to the tips of every part
that's still alive. The tree shudders and cracks, opens its
heart with stiff unpractised art its soul begins to flow as
sun-kissed love prepares it now to flow and stream to
soften its stiff cold sticks with ecstasy and life. The
fundamental goal of all live things that makes them want
to live and sing and flower too is love's warmth and
tender touch that gave in selfless natural joy would
move a stone and change a mountainside to soft

heather-filled hills, bleak moor to forest charged with
tumultuous song and rife with flowers of all kind to stun
the mind and give its brilliance to all mankind. So tree,
come back to life and budge your life force by a kiss that
it will give you, soft caress, warm silken touch, like
mother's gentle nudge on newborn cub. The sun gives
all so much, will not miss you but loves you most of all
since you poor withered thing alone and torn need all
the love and warmth that it can give. So arise and wear
your crest, your coat of arms, be proud. Thrust up your
head into the clouds. Open your massive branches and
let them be sanctuary for all tired things to rest on and
to buzz and sing. You are a king. Your crown, your shimmering
display of whispering green your glittering sheen. So
when the autumn comes dear friendly tree and sun
withdraws its love and ecstasy then winter breaks your
heart as love seems to depart forever. Do not fret like
some poor broken love-sick poet in his winter room but
know that love will come again to warm you. Will again
arrive but only can ignite your precious soul if you
believe in your power to receive its love and stay alive.

Actor

Greeting, hallo John, hallo Richard and how are you?
Hallo Mike
How are you?
Working?
Really that's good
What are you doing?
A play
How really fine
See you
Have a nice day
Hallo Peter how are you?
I'm doing well too
Working?
You are?
That's good
Bastard he couldn't act his way out of a paper bag
The slag
Still I'll show them
Those out there
The faceless ones
The ones in the chairs
They haven't got the guts to get out there
Hallo darling
You're lovely
You really are
I think our fates are designed in the stars

You're divine
Yes I do really take this woman to be really mine
Get the kettle on love
It's nearly nine
Hallo ma this is…
Great just great
Getting on fine

Just watch this space
So why couldn't they get you a commercial or two?
Sorry ma
That's not what I had in view
For me
That's for the others
Not men of quality
I saw you last week on the TV
An astronaut
But couldn't see your face
I rang Auntie Betty
She raced to the set but when she got there
It was off the air
Bye ma
Yes darling of course I'm as happy
How can you doubt
I haven't kissed you in weeks?
Sometimes you forget
Stop nagging I'm trying to work on my text
If I don't work soon
I don't exist
That's a feeling these days that tends to persist
Hallo John
How are you?
You working?
Oh
I'm glad that you're pulling through
I'm glad to hear that all your efforts are beginning to bear
Fruit
Is that the word?
Fred how are you?
You working for TV?
Directing, oh that's cool.
Then don't forget me
Ha Ha
Your old chum from school

How did he…
He flogged his bum
Succeed
That weed?
Joined that club
The faceless ones
All rub shoulders in the bar
The ones who can't do it
The ones in the chairs
The ones who say thank you and who is next?
Hallo darling
Had a nice day?
Yeah I did nothing
Walked streets and sat in cafés
Get a job?!
I'm an actor, you bitch
Got to be free
Got to be fit
No one phoned
Are you sure?
You were all day
At home?
Hallo John
You working?
You are, that's good
You'll go far
Acts like wood
Hallo Jack
What's new?
Nothing
Aah tough
Things will improve
The going is rough
Remember at RADA what they said my dear
If you want to be a star you have to persevere
If you want to be top of the shit heap

You mustn't complain
If your shoes stink of turds at the end of the day
Hallo darling
What's your name?
You're lovely you are
I love you for ever
You're what I'm looking for
You keep the TV
I'll keep the car
We'll sell the house
Can't stand no more
Hallo Joe
I'm doing great
Up for series?
Not yet
Short list
Near as damn it
I'll get you a guest
Spot
If you like
My agent's talking money
Then it's sewn up
Hallo darling, sure I love you
Hold on there's the phone
Did I?
No
Sure, there'll be other parts
The bastards don't give me the shit from their ass
Hallo ma
Hallo pa
How are things?
I've seen nothing but rubbish on TV
Why aren't you there son?
You look like Paul Newman
Doesn't he dear?
Hallo dad

Don't talk to me you parasite
You bum
All you can do is scrounge when you come
Yeah! I'll be keeping you one day
You old cunt
Don't talk to your father like that
Be a son
That we can be proud of
Whenever we speak
I've got an audition
I swear next week
To be
Or not to be that is the question whether 'tis nobler in the
mind
To be the slings and arrows of outrageous fortune
Thank you that's enough
We'll let you know
We'll contact your agent
Please don't phone
Yes darling was great
The money will flow
So what I've not made love in a month
What's in your head romance and bullshit that's for me
dead
Then go
Fuck off
Sorry I wed
You
Hallo Richard
You doing well?
You doing a movie?
Fucking hell
No I'm not that smart
You've got a good agent
Mine's just a fart
Anything going?

Any more parts
That require my stunning talent
Oh, it's all cast
Bastard
Wont give you the shit from his ass
Hallo did I get the job?
Didn't think I was right
Cunts
I could act the pants off the slobs
Theatre
It's full of the dead
They rake the graveyards
The lousy shitheads
They're walking corpses
Little blind mice
Rats in armchairs
Hallo she hung up
Hallo darling I'm back home
Dear John
Sorry I really must go
Sorry to leave like this
I just got so
Bored with the life
Bored with the fight that must go on
Day and Night
Don't forget to feed pussy
Please don't write
I'll find better than you
Go
I don't care
You got no guts
I won't shed a tear
Hallo John
How are you, working?
No
Good

I mean good you're not dead
It's good that you
Hold on
Hold on to your soul
Or take arms against a sea of troubles and by opposing
end them
To die to sleep no more and by a sleep to say we end
the heartache
Thank you we'll let you know
And please
We do ask you not to phone
Do I have a chance?
Tell me?
You can tell me now if I'm not the right one
Then I'd
We're thinking about it
Call in the next
Hallo ma
Hallo pa
No got no dough
Lend me a fiver just to get through
I need a few bob
Times will improve
He looks like Paul Newman doesn't he Al?
He looks like a ponce
Go to hell
He'll show them
I will
I'll smash through
I'll show them what talent is
I'll break ducking through
Hallo darling
You're lovely
You look like a peach
You're really divine
Any commercials even?

Will you be mine?
My wife ran off with a telephone line
There must be something
I think we're made for each other
Like fate
No I don't exude hate
I love the bastards
I'm all sweet and charm
Alright I'll lick ass
All greasy and smarm
She hung up
Hallo John
You working?
You are?
Where?
Show me
I'll be a star
Yet
Fuck you
You pigs
You bare your asses
You untalented shits
Shit gathered together in one bowl
I'll flush you away
Give me a role
What do you mean cancer?
Yeah I'll try and get round
Yeah that word has an ugly sound
Who would fardels bear to grunt and sweat under a
weary life that the fear of something after death
Hallo darling I love you!
Oh, leave me alone
I've got other problems
So fuck off, just go
You fed up with me
Women like you they grow on

Ma don't die
Don't go just yet
Don't leave me just now
I'm starring in
Hamlet
I think you'll be proud
What did she say?
Her last words
Before she passed away
You look like Paul Newman and have a nice day
Goodbye ma and pa
I'll cry at your grave
But I've got an audition I mustn't be late
Whether it is nobler in the mind to suffer the slings and
arrows of outrageous fortune
Thank you very much
We'll let you know
Please call your agent
Please don't phone
Hallo
Did they want?
No
Why?
I have to know
Get the fucking kid out of here
I'm on the phone
She hung up again, oh no
Hallo John
What's new?
How's tricks?
Yeah terrific
I do bits
And pieces
Maybe Hamlet
Too old
I'm an actor you prick

Hallo darling I'm home
What's this?
Couldn't stand any more
Don't be upset husband
Don't be sore
Just couldn't stand it anymore
Need peace for the kids
You can see them of course
Say once a month
We'll discuss it in court
Get a job and I'm sure you'll find
At the end
Peace of mind
You're mad
I'm tough
The others are assholes and creeps
Pigs at a trough
Hallo Jack
Hallo Frank
How's graft?
Read your reviews?
You're doing good
You're smart
A good agent
That gives you the start
Yeah, I'm great
Got to fly
Mustn't be late
To be or not to be that is the question
Whether 'tis nobler in the mind to bear the slings and
arrows of outrageous fortune
Outrageous fortune
To die
To sleep
No more and by a sleep to say we end the heart
Ache.................. Maaaaaaa!!

Black Skater

I saw you big black man rolling down Venice Strip the
vein of land where skaters slide across your eyes their
sculptured hips.
I saw your brutal force packed strong like a huge mighty
Rodin sculpture in a thong or nylon leotard and pants.
I must suppress a smile, your elegance not wilted down,
no not a bit by dropping your shoulder strap letting it,
sway by your rib cage. Your cowboy hat white socks and
boots careering softly down, a floating cappuccino in white
and brown displaying your black and narcissistic flower
in Venice town. You slid so softly happy in your prime.
Like some big steak for us to dine our eyes on
make a feast of this black fantasy, black Samson
rollerskating majesty. You would say hi! to him
hallo! to her. Familiar faces grin would be demure to your
huge grace roller skating Californian black ace.
Yet when I followed your progress with English eyes in
wonderment under the US skies of what more marvels
can this country show? What wealth of fantastic and
gaudy show to starved eyes of Europe's yellow face?
The limpid dying fast decaying race so when this Marco
Polo journeying far like some wild errant shooting star
did see these giants from the colonies, these sights,
these wondrous healthy Los Angelenos he could only
stare like some poor orphan for the first time at a fair
where everything was heaven to his hungry look.
Everything was the most fantastic book of wonders
yet in spite of all, in spite of all this crashing display of
wealth in muscle satin fantasy I saw you pulling out your
shorts where they had crept up in your arse the way they
do a little tight. They tend to crawl right, into your crack
not quite so smart to be half up your arse so this small
gesture multiplied so many times your fingers pulling
shorts down to the thighs did make you just a popcorn

king not mighty King Kong any more but puffed up
swollen little boy of four and up and down your skates
would take your mighty feet by end of evening when the
sun went down the mighty Samson had become a
chocolate clown.

Action

I write too much I say the same old thing I must keep
now my mouth and mind in chains I must learn to say
less and do more let action say what words can only
touch and bounce away. Action gives real evidence
of the day. So shut your trap and open up our heart.
Make motion and then you have a start to finish or
without the action you will change your mind since words
are easy, never bind. You write the one day what the
next you leave behind so sit and think and then you
stake the claim to shove one foot in front another and
then again so action takes you to the place when words
would only that replace.

California Morn

See how beautiful is the sky thrown across the mountain
with a trowel or the furrowed earth scooped and torn
or scudding across the morning dawn like chariots of fire
pierced with the sun's bright horns. The damp earth
rained through the velvet night smells like new bread
soft and warm the blue-stained hills cut out in silhouette
against the sky which drops its gouache of eau de nil or
baby blue, depending on the light that rises over the
green belly of the sea mirrored in tearful grey and misty.
Sometimes like curds sometimes like whey
small pools, torn handkerchiefs of sky fell down like
flaked plaster in the windy night and left their paint in
puddles that dried returning to repatch the tears in the
great blue tented sky. The music oozes its confection of
heart and ache into the morning air tingeing it sweet and
colouring the sound of morning voices where people sit
and eat. Golden rivers flood white oval plates with eggs
and toast and thin sliced potato flakes The cool fresh
tangy soft light sweet morning wind caresses my face
and flits around each jutting cliff each precipice, round
brow and nose then curves and filters down the cheeks,
circling each nostril then sweeps and howls around my
jaw, tickles a whisper like a spume of smoke inside my
ear and pats farewell until the next silk breath of wind
appears. Cycles thinly wheel their tracks making small
cricket sounds as urgent thighs like cables of fine steel
pound their oily sweaty pistons up and down. They
gradually dissolve into the receding light that sucks each thing
that enters it and taking little bites and now it smaller
grows, now tiny, now a fleck a barely moving particle and
gulp it all flows. It all comes and goes, cause now just as
your eye gave up the chase on bicycle that waved and
danced its way and then to your chagrin escaped. Well
now a dot begins to grow a spit of colour, fuzzy, now it

starts to shape and from its globe small spikes appear,
and lines now do define that where the bike had
disappeared into the hungry lion, it vomited back into
your eye a moving piece of life. I turned my eye away
onto my golden plate which then appeared my eggs all
warm did flow and like pure molten lava glowed
or as LA's giant rolling hills, the eggs did o'er the snow
white plate tumble and spill, the ketchup in its bottle
gleamed all bright, rich ruby red. I gripped, twisted its
metal cap, poured out its saucy blood. It plunked,
globbed down and splashed the egg which now
wounded did seem as fork and knife slashed, dug and
cut and scooped my breakfast feast. Ooh crumble,
smear the golden rye with thick rich drooling *beurre*
and gather eggy nuggets on the toast so there would be
a crush of tastes swilling round my tongue while in my
other hand I grabbed a cup of coffee, poured it down.
The dot that now appeared waving and bobbing growing
larger by each stride, expanding in the centre of my eye,
now was filling up the space now growing larger with
each pace. A runner eating up the air, advancing.
Soon it will appear with a puff and pound his head and
chest now leaping up and down and left and right as if
the earth shook him from side to side. He lacked the
grace of sinewed muscle in its holy state obeying rhymes
so intricate to make a body seem to float in space but
like a puppet dangling from its strings held by a drunken
master so it seemed. He thrust his head this way and
that as if his nerves and muscle were at war each
struggling to obey a different drum. His limbs threshed,
struck the ground beneath his withered steps which sent
shocks to his trunks which spun away as if a mighty fist
had punched and made him sway. Just then this body
sculptured from his waist of rippling embroidery of
muscle to his face so etched in pain, I saw the reason for
his ungainly shape when on two crutches he attempts his

tortured race his bravery did move us all. Our knives and forks stood still. Our hearts moved more.

His withered limbs so shrunk were as two twigs, his feet dragged just as if... no feeling flooded through those useless legs and all his might did rest on those two wooden pegs which hit the hard cement and pushed him through. Then once again he lifted up his oars, dragged up to sink once more into his daily hard routine to run like any other human, keep his dignity in jerky ugly jog but now to me it was his soul that flared from out of his pain. His morning early tryst, his tortured face because this poor valiant man ignored the unfair stroke that shattered what we have. So naturally to be blessed with sympathy of muscle, brain and nerve to move each separate digit to the inspiration like a bird. I saw him dance away into the distant swarm. His hopping gait. His grimace filled my eye and warned us all who once again stuffed mouths with eggs and coffee and gain of the frustration that we do ourselves complain that here was love that overcame the desperate misfortune and hurt and turned it into blinding inspiration that must burn into our self-satisfied and greedy smirk.

Baby Talk

To be a single mother, horrific task schlepping round
collapsible pram, filthy shit inside the house banal low
talk and puking brats. The house is now a nursery, your
mind scrambled by iglee gee. The mother once a lovely
dame perfect, careless, sweet and game not sorrowed
brow, smelly muck fingers, not clean and freshly white,
but now this monster,
this foul id came bursting out in screaming shit-producing
howl. Tender, sweet woman now is fouled heartbroke
crying, up all night career and freedom to express
the soul in the world's mirror cracked a hole now torn from
out her garden her dazzling display, she threw seeds
there one day and had ambitions to see a colourful array
but now she schleps collapsible pram to café.
Struggles to get out the house no one, husband fucked
off the louse so she in need departs her toy-strewed
muck-heap room that once was planned in care, a white
cocoon. Zen temple for her mind to meditate on poetry
and life. And now a garbage heap, plastic consumer
games for howling brats to make them tame. Baby's now
to blame. A ball of energy and flaming life. I don't deny its
need to bite upon the nipple of the world. Its miracle is
joy to motherhood. It's pure, complete, we are like Gods
to make a piece of human with our mate but I can learn
to love as hate, all humans do. I love the golden stream
of light that becomes this stinking sprawling mite. This
baby talk, this howl, this sheik, this gimme, gimme.
Don't want a wooden doll. Don't want a quiet deadly
thing. I want a child to cry and sing. I want a child to be.
It's only what I see in urban hell. Bedsitter in the grey
damp smell of city life. A single lonely woman in her
painful strife in grey-filled days. Social security and long
queue for her small gratuity pushing the pram and sitting
in launderettes as her life's dream grows less and less.

She is still young. A child herself with dreams unfilled like
a stocking Santa misses. Young woman once so soft
and yielding to a man who promised the world at least do
what he can. Would hold up half his share and more but
soon found it a bloody bore. Decides to paint by soft
Ibizan shores. Leave his woman, "I must be free." My soul
untrammelled by responsibility I'll send some cash he
says, "when I can but now must be a single man" so
ageing hippy lets his young wife take the can. So here in
Hampstead, Sunday drear, the coffee house is crowded
and one small dear baby on one arm the other gripping
pram looks for a chair to rest her aching hams. She sits,
she's all relieved, she's out. Her goal achieved, she's
whole again. Once more in the old coffee house she
liked when she was single unworn strife but then it
crowds up now. Her table's packed with four friends
chatting loud. She's squeezed away, their elbows push
and shove. Her little space has no protection but must
shrink. No man to hold a space for her to think. So up
she gets and schleps the pram again. It collapses in the
street. It rains, always as if the pain of England sheds its
never-ending teardrops every day. Off she walks back to
her room, back to her unrelenting gloom.
At least she had her coffee.
Had her Sunday walk.
And now… baby talk!